Laughter to Lighten the Load

Uplifting Reminders and Funny Photos
To Help You Keep a Sense of Humor

Inspired by Faith

Laughter to Lighten the Load
©Product Concept Mfg., Inc.

Laughter to Lighten the Load
ISBN 978-0-9909508-9-9
Published by Product Concept Mfg., Inc.
2175 N. Academy Circle #200, Colorado Springs, CO 80909

Written and Compiled by Linda Staten with contributions
by Patricia Mitchell and Vicki J. Kuyper in association
with Product Concept Mfg., Inc.

All scripture quotations are from the King James version
of the Bible unless otherwise noted.

Scriptures taken from the Holy Bible,
New International Version®, NIV®.
Copyright © 1973, 1978, 1984 by Biblica, Inc.™
Used by permission of Zondervan.
All rights reserved worldwide.
www.zondervan.com

Sayings not having a credit listed are contributed by writers
for Product Concept Mfg., Inc. or in a rare case,
the author is unknown.

Laughter to Lighten the Load

Let thine heart be merry.

Judges 19:6

If you've ever misplaced your sense of humor under a pile of laundry…if you've ever wanted a breather, a get-away, a stress-buster, or just a few moments to let go of your worries and feel like a carefree kid again (instead of the impressively responsible grown up you are)…if you've ever needed a laugh to lighten the load, this book is for you.

We are never too old or too
young to laugh.

When you count your blessings,
don't forget to count your sense
of humor.

You cannot truly
live life fully
if you cannot laugh.

Honk if you love squirrels.

A Nutty Tale

A squirrel walked into a fast food place and asked, "Do you have any nuts?"

The manager said "no", and the squirrel left.

The next day the squirrel returned and asked, "Do you have any nuts?"

The manager said in a loud voice, "No!", and the squirrel scurried out.

The next day, the squirrel walked in the door and asked, "Do you have any nuts?"

The frustrated manager began to yell. "No! And if you come in here one more time asking for nuts, I'm going to glue your fuzzy tail to the front door!" The squirrel hopped out.

The next day, the squirrel came back.

"What did I tell you?" the manager asked angrily.

The squirrel looked at him and said, "Do you have any glue?"

"Why, no," the puzzled manager replied.

"Then do you have any nuts?"

Fun Fact

Researchers have found that when you laugh, the movement involved will exercise your heart, your abs and your diaphragm. Not only that, but you'll burn extra calories.

Just imagine a gym where all you do is laugh! Who wouldn't want a lifetime membership? Plus, you wouldn't have to wear those stretchy little outfits, either!

Laughter is Good Exercise

I've tried all the machines at the gym, but the only one I keep using is the vending machine.

When I signed up for exercise classes, they said to wear loose-fitting clothes. If your clothes are loose, why do you need to sign up for an exercise class?

Instead of exercise class, I decided to diet for fourteen days. All I lost was two weeks.

Time Machine

A mother and her daughter were visiting the big city for the very first time.

They walked into the lobby of a sky-scraper, and watched as two metal doors parted and an elderly man entered. The doors closed behind him.

A few minutes later, they watched in amazement as the doors parted again, and a young, handsome man stepped out.

"Come on, sweetie," the mother said. "I want to go fetch your father and see if he'll get in that machine."

You can discover more about
a person in an hour of play than in a
year of conversation.

Plato

Laugh yourself into stitches.
William Shakespeare

The most wasted day of all
is that in which we have not laughed.

Nicolas Chamfort

Hey, wait a minute.
I'm the one who takes
the catnaps around here!

A Few Thoughts about Cats

- Cats don't have owners.
  They have staff.

- There is no snooze button
  on a hungry kitten.

- Cats have no doubt they
  are a-mewsing.

- Cats know how to find the sunny side
  of life…and nap in it.

A Few Thoughts about Dogs

- A lazy dog only chases parked cars.

- Dogs have lots of friends because
they wag their tails and not their tongues.

- Dogs are comforting because when you
feel blue, they don't ask why.

- You can tell when a dog is getting old.
He fetches yesterday's paper.

When life gets a little trying,
try a little laughter.

Burdens become light when cheerfully borne.
Ovid

Laughter...it's like a tiny vacation
your heart takes.

Home on the Range

Out on the lone prairie, several buffalo were grazing when a surly cowboy rode up alongside them. He stopped his horse and glared at them for several minutes. Then he spat on the ground.

"You want to know my opinion?" he said. "I think you're the ugliest critters I've ever seen." With that, the cowboy turned and rode off.

One buffalo languidly turned to his companions and said, "Fellas, I think we just heard a discouraging word."

And the buffalo nodded in agreement and kept on grazing contentedly.

Did you hear the one about the
two cowboys who went to a fancy restaurant
for bison steaks?

*When they were finished eating,
they didn't have enough money to pay
the buffalo bill.*

Two cows were in a pasture
when a milk truck passed by.

The advertising on the side said,
"Homogenized! Pasteurized!
Vitamin A added!"

*"Kinda makes you feel inadequate,
doesn't it?" remarked one cow to the other.*

I see you got my tweet!

Two things to help you
deal with life's ups and downs:
A good deal of faith,
and a good sense of humor.

We're all here for a spell;
get all the good laughs you can.
Will Rogers

A light heart lives long.
William Shakespeare

Family Flattery

At a family gathering, an elderly aunt asked her young nephew to guess her age. He hesitated to answer, so she said with a teasing smile, "You have some idea how old I am, don't you?"

"Well, yes, I do," the nephew replied, "but I don't know whether to make it ten years younger because of your appearance, or ten years older because of your intelligence."

MYOB

A mom working in her backyard one spring day saw her elderly neighbor out puttering in her yard.

"Bobby," she called to her son. Go next door and see how old Mrs. Harris is."

He left and returned a few minutes later.

"She seems fine, but she's mad at you," Bobby reported.

"Why?" the mom asked.

"She said it was none of your business how old she is."

Here's Looking at You

A man moved into a retirement community. He noticed one woman who was always looking at him.

Finally curiosity got the better of him, and he walked over to the woman and asked her why she was always looking at him so intently.

"It's because you look like my third husband," she told him.

"Oh, I see," said the man. "How many times have you been married?"

"Twice," she replied.

Those who tickle themselves can laugh
when they please.

Proverb

*There is no duty we so much underrate
as the duty of being happy.*

Robert Louis Stevenson

When mama's happy,
everybody's happy.
(Mama said it so it must be true!)

He who laughs last probably
    doesn't get the joke.

Puppy Love

The animal lover next door was out in her backyard, cleaning the koi pond. Her dogs were all around her.

"Hi," the neighbor shouted over the fence. "I see you've got your whole family with you."

"Well, almost. My husband's not here," the animal lover replied a bit wistfully.

"Oh. How come?"

"He told me I had to choose. It was either him or the dogs," she replied. "I miss him sometimes."

Fun Fact

Studies have shown that newborn babies begin smiling as soon as two hours after they make their grand entrance into the world.

Tea Party

A toddler was having a tea party for her father. She brought him little cups of water which served as pretend tea. Her father acted very thirsty and drank several cups. He thought it was adorable.

When her mother came home, the father told her all about the tea party, and how cute their daughter was, carefully carrying those little play cups of "tea". The little girl brought one last cup to her daddy. He drank it down and smiled at his wife.

She smiled back, and said, "You do know that the only place she can reach water is the toilet."

If you've made a child giggle,
it's been a good day.

*Even the most serious person
cannot remain that way
when there's a laughing baby in the room.*

Mix a little foolishness
with your serious plans. It is lovely to be
silly at the right moment.

Horace

Are we having fun yet?

Dad was teaching his daughter how to drive. Suddenly she screamed, "Dad, here comes a utility pole! What do I do now?"

One weekend, a husband and wife decided they'd like to get away from it all... so they loaded the car with children, snacks, pets, suitcases, toys, computer games, coloring books...

Mom Wisdom

A mother mouse and her little one were strolling in the sunshine when suddenly the neighborhood tomcat sprang in front of them and snarled. Mom mouse stopped, stood as tall as she could, and bellowed, "Woof! Woof! Woof!" The stunned tom turned tail and scampered away.

"See?" Mom said to her little one as they continued their walk. "That's why it's so important to learn a second language!"

Dad Wisdom

Jimmy came home one day with a black eye.

"Did you get into a fight?" his father said. "Don't you remember how I told you to count to ten before you lose your temper?"

"I did, but Tommy's dad told him to count to five, so he hit me first!"

No, I said my name is Sue.
Not sushi!

Fish Tale

Around the water cooler, a fishing enthusiast was boasting to his coworkers about the 15-pound salmon he had landed that weekend.

"Now wait a minute!" a coworker interrupted, "were there any witnesses?"

"Yes, there were," the fisher replied, "otherwise that salmon would have weighed 25 pounds!"

So Many Ways to Laugh

Have you ever noticed how many ways there are to laugh, and how many words we have to describe them? Sure, we can simply laugh. But we can also chuckle, chortle, giggle, guffaw, snicker, snort and lots of other things.

That's because laughter is a response to many different things – to a joke, a look, a favorite family story, silly things that people and animals do, and unexpected thing that tickle our minds or catch our hearts off-guard. No wonder we respond in so many different ways.

We're complicated creatures. That can make even a simple thing like laughter complicated as well! But it's also a reason we humans really need laughter in our lives.

Laughter is like a prayer of thanks,
telling God how happy His world makes us.

You have as much laughter as you have faith.
Martin Luther

God hath made me to laugh, so that all that
hear will laugh with me.
Genesis 21:6

Church Signs

- God loves knee-mail.

- This building is prayer-conditioned.

- We specialize in faith lifts.

- Seven days without church makes one weak.

- Give God what's right, not what's left.

- Forbidden fruits create many jams.

- What's missing from ch ch? U R

- Need a lifeguard? Ours walks on water.

- If you're the one who keeps praying for snow, please stop.

- If your life stinks, we have a pew.

- Have trouble sleeping? We have sermons.

Prayer Meeting

Out in the African bush, a missionary was being chased by a lion. Finding himself cornered, he dropped to his knees and begged God for deliverance. To his surprise, the lion also started to pray.

"This really is a miracle," the missionary exclaimed to the lion. "Here you are, joining me in prayer just when I thought you were going to kill me!"

"Shhhh," replied the lion. "I'm saying grace."

Heaven-Bound

In church on Sunday morning, a preacher delivered a sermon on the glories of heaven. In conclusion, he shouted to his congregants, "Will everyone who wants to go to heaven please stand up!" Everyone rose from their pew except one man. The pastor noticed, and at the end of the service asked the man, "Are you telling me you *don't* want to go to heaven?"

Of course I want to go to heaven," the man answered.

"Then why didn't you stand up when everyone else did?"

"Because I thought you might be planning a trip there this afternoon."

The art of being happy lies
in the power of extracting happiness
from common things.

Henry Ward Beecher

Every now and then,
go away and have a little relaxation…
to remain constantly at work
will diminish your judgment.

Leonardo da Vinci

Man is the only animal that laughs and
weeps; for he is the only animal that is
struck with the difference between what
things are, and what they ought to be.

William Hazlitt

You know you're getting older when...

- you have a party and your neighbors don't know it

- you hear your favorite songs in elevators

- your back goes out more often than you do

- your grandkids ask what those stripey things are under your eyes

- you learn to appreciate what is... before it isn't."

Mirth is God's medicine.

Henry Ward Beecher

A good laugh and a long sleep
are the best cures in the doctor's book.

Proverb

Laugh till your soul gets thoroughly rested.

Josh Billings

Take Your Medicine

Laughter is good medicine.
Some say that it's the best.
Now if you don't believe that,
you can put it to the test.
Next time you're feeling frowny
or your world looks kinda grey,
find something that will bring a laugh
to turn around your day.

Hold a little family contest
making funny faces.
Watch a silly movie
or go out to happy places.
A dose of grins and giggles
every day and every night
will keep your attitude in shape,
and make your heart feel light.

Are you sure line dancing is still in?

Why do cars like hip-hop music?
They can brake dance.

What dance did the Pilgrims do?
The Plymouth Rock.

How many dance instructors does it take to
change a lightbulb?
Five!...Six!...Seven!...Eight!

Fun Fact

Studies of people who live to be a hundred years old have shown some not-so-surprising results. When asked the secret to their longevity, centenarians often credit their sense of humor.

If you don't learn to laugh at trouble,
you won't have anything to laugh
at when you're old.

Edgar Watson Howe

With mirth and laughter
let old wrinkles come.

William Shakespeare

I know not all that may be coming,
but be it what it will,
I'll go to it laughing.

Herman Melville

Grizzly Lesson

"You need to laugh more," one grizzly said.

"Sure, yeah," the other grizzly replied.

"Really! You need to laugh more," the grizzly said again.

"I heard you the first time," the other one responded.

"No, I mean it. You need to laugh more," the grizzly insisted.

"Why do you keep telling me that?" the other grizzly shouted.

"Good advice just bears repeating."

Everyone talks about lowbrow humor
and highbrow humor.
But what about unibrow humor?

Sometimes when you least expect it,
life sneaks up and tickles you.

Laughter.
It's the universal language.

Everyone needs a friend
    to horse around with.
(And laugh at their corny jokes!)

Lighthearted

Affirming

Uplifting

Genuine

Healing

Transforming

Engaging

Renewing

Laughter Can Change the World

We have experienced in our lifetime occasions when the whole world unites in a moment of silence or a moment of prayer. What if we all had a moment of laughter? What if everyone everywhere stopped whatever they were doing one certain day to share a joke or a story or a goofy picture? Imagine it.

Everyone smiling and laughing, no one bored or lonely or unhappy. No one hurt or hurting anyone else.

And when that moment of laughter was over, the world would probably never be the same again.

Safety First

The little boy was helping his grandma put away the groceries. His grandma looked over and saw him open the box of animal crackers and carefully examine the animals, one by one.

"What on earth are you doing?" she asked.

It says on the box that you shouldn't eat them if the seal is broken," her grandson explained, "so I'm looking for the seal."

The Power of Prayer

Two terrified skunks were running as fast as they could to get away from a hound that was chasing them through the forest. When they came upon a third skunk, they yelled, "Quick! Run! A dog is after us!"

"Calm down, fellas, calm down," the third skunk told them. As the other two looked at him in amazement, he bowed his head and said, "Let us spray."

Fun at the Movies

A man in a movie theater notices what looks like a skunk sitting next to him.

"Oh, my goodness, are you a skunk?" asked the shocked man.

"Yes."

"What are you doing in this theater?"

"Well, I liked the book," the skunk replied.

Mysterious Questions

What can you hold without ever touching it?
Your breath.

What question can never be
answered with "yes"?
"Are you asleep?"

Which runs faster, hot or cold?
Hot, because you can catch cold.

What's the invention that lets you see
through the thickest walls?
A window.

Weather alert!
It's raining cats and dogs.
Watch out for poodles.

Look On the Bright Side

Two women were out walking when the sky darkened and it began to pour down rain.

"It's raining cats and dogs," one woman said as they ran for cover.

"But at least it's not hailing cabs," the other woman replied.

Someone could use a harebrush.
Just saying.

When rabbits are unhappy, what do they do?
They read the bunny papers.
(Groan!)

Why did the rabbit family decide
to buy a house?
They were just tired of the hole thing!

What do you get when you cross a rabbit
with a leaf blower?
A hare dryer.

Kidding Around

When we laugh and enjoy ourselves, we often say we're "just kidding around". There's a good reason for that. Children know how to have fun, and they believe it's a really important part of life. In fact, they devote most of their waking moments to the pursuit of smiles and laughter. As they get older, adults tell them to stop kidding around and grow up. And they become us.

But wouldn't it be nice if we could become them a little more often, if we could retrieve that wisdom we possessed as children and make guilt-free time now and then— between work and chores and errands and paying bills—to just kid around?

Why did the man climb to the
roof of the restaurant?
They told him his meal was on the house.

A restaurant is the only place where people
are happy when they're fed up.

"Waiter, how long have you worked here?"
a diner asked.
"About a year, sir," the waiter replied.
"Oh, then it couldn't be you
who took my order."

Fresh Perspective

Four restaurants opened on different corners of the same block.

The owner of the first eatery put up a sign claiming "Best Restaurant in the City!"

The owner of the second put up a larger sign declaring "Best Restaurant in the Country!"

The owner of the third put up an even larger sign proclaiming "Best Restaurant in the Whole World!"

The owner of the fourth walked around the block, looking at the three signs. The next morning a sign appeared on the front of his establishment: "Best Restaurant on This Block."

Signs of the Times

In a health food store window:
Closed due to illness

In an office building:
Toilet out of order. Please use floor below.

In a department store:
Bargain Basement Upstairs

On a traffic barrier:
Please don't hit me again.

On a maternity ward door:
Push. Push. Push.

On an ice cream shop:
Our gelato won't let you down
but it will dessert you.

We all have things in life that just plain puzzle us

Take these phrases, for example:

Jumbo shrimp.

Pretty ugly.

Mute sound.

Definite maybe.

Unlimited budget.

Old news.

Golf fashion.

Objective opinion.

Near future.

Worst favorite.

Numb feeling.

Inherited debt.

Same difference.

Genuine imitation.

Extremely average.

Small miracle.

I'm speechless.
  You took the words right out of my mouth.

One morning two hens were pecking in the yard.

Suddenly a softball appeared from over the fence and landed with a plop! right next to them.

"Well, Biddy is a bit of a show-off!" one hen gasped to the other.

"Look at what she's laying next door!"

You're too much into technology if...

- your laptop costs more than your car.

- during plane trips you keep your laptop on your lap and stow your kids under the seat.

- you get up during the night to use the bathroom, then check your email and social network page before going back to bed.

Modern Parenting

A frustrated dad described to one of his coworkers his teen son's take-it or leave-it attitude toward homework and household chores.

"When I was his age," the dad said, "my father would send me to my room for a couple of hours of time out. But in my son's room, there's a tv, computer, game console and music system."

"So what do you do?" the coworker asked.

"I send him to my room," the dad smiled.

Laughing Stock

Laughter is a dividend that comes from investing your time and your feelings wisely. Find reasons to be happy, even on days when it takes some extra searching.

Know who you are, and don't be afraid to laugh at yourself now and then. Always allow a few moments each day to feel like a kid again. If you hear a hilarious story or a corny joke, share it with someone you love.

The more you invest in your own cheerfulness and delight, the more you can give to others.

When it comes to laughing stock, there are many options. Be sure to include in your portfolio a wide range of giggles, guffaws, chuckles, snickers, roars, tee hees, and ha ha ha's.

And remember, when you laugh, those around you will laugh, well-being will increase, and your laughing stock can only rise in value. The gift of laughter is priceless. Invest wisely and often!

There is a stereotype
that women aren't funny.
The only people who believe that
are those who have never been
to a girls' night out.

Some people we laugh with,
and some people we cry with,
but if we have people
we can do both with
that's really the best of all.

"Ha ha! You're such a ham."
        "And you quack me up!"

What do you get when you cross
a pig and a cactus?
A porky-pine.

Why should you never tell a pig a secret?
They squeal.

Who is the smartest pig in the world?
Ein-swine.

Babysitting

A teenaged boy was watching his baby sister while their parents were out. He decided to go fishing, and took her along.

"I'll never do that again," the big brother said at the dinner table that evening.

"Why not?' his mother asked. "Did she make so much noise that she scared away the fish?"

"No," replied the boy. "She ate every last bit of my bait!"

Laughter is a joyful noise.
(Make it!)

One joy scatters a hundred griefs.
Proverb

Be glad of life
because it gives you the chance
to love and to work and to play
and to look up at the stars.
Henry Van Dyke

Big Deal

A man came home one day and announced to his wife that he had been promoted.

"To what?" she asked.

"To vice president of the company!" the man proudly stated.

"Oh, that's nice," his wife replied.

"It's not just nice. It's a really big deal!" the husband insisted.

"Well," said the wife, "I don't know about that. At the supermarket there's a vice president of everything – of dairy, canned goods, produce. There's even a vice-president of prunes."

Now the husband had been in business a long time, and he knew that people loved fancy titles, but this was just too hard to believe.

"What's the number of that grocery store?" The wife dialed it and handed the phone to her husband.

"Hello. May I please speak with the vice president of prunes," the husband asked as he rolled his eyes.

"Packaged or bulk?" the clerk inquired.

Sing-along

Why couldn't the bell keep a secret?
Because it always tolled.

How do you make a bandstand?
Take away all their chairs.

How many folksingers does it take
to change a lightbulb?
*One to change it, and five to sing about how
good the old one was.*

What do you get if you drop
a piano into a mineshaft?
A Flat Miner.

Fun Fact

Laughter helps strengthen relationships. That's because sharing a laugh with someone triggers an instant emotional connection. Letting another person know what you find funny is open and honest. We tend to laugh much more often with people we trust, with people we feel we can show our real selves to.

Think about it. Who are the people you laugh with most often or most freely, the people you turn to when you need cheering up, the people who "get" you – and your sense of humor?

I'm so cute you might want
to dog-ear this page!

What is a puppy's favorite treat?
A funny bone.

Why are dogs poor dancers?
They have two left feet.

Why do dogs run in circles?
Because it's too hard to run in squares.

School Daze

A shamefaced student approached her teacher.

"Miss Smith," she said, "you wouldn't punish me for something I didn't do, would you?"

"Well, of course not!" the teacher replied.

The student's face brightened. "Oh, thank you so much," she gushed, "because I didn't do my homework."

You Had to Ask

A teacher posed a question to her young pupils:

"If you had a dollar, and you asked your dad for another dollar, what would you have?"

Billy raised his hand and answered: "One dollar."

"Billy, I'm afraid you don't know your math." Billy said, "Teacher, you don't know my dad."

If you could herd cats, what would you have?
A *purr-ade*.
(*But don't waste your time trying!*)

What do you call a cat who laughs at you?
A *gigglepuss*.

It's a little known fact, but most cats are
highly educated. No lion!
*They study mewsic, hisstory
and fureign languages.*

What does a cat call a hummingbird?
Fast food.

Dog Owner's Prayer

God, help me to become
the person my dog thinks I am.

Cat Owner's Prayer

God help me.

Tick-Tock

A woman had a hard time getting up in the morning, and on most mornings, she was at least an hour late getting to her job. Her boss told her that she would lose her job if this continued, so she went to see her physician about the problem. Armed with a sleeping pill, she went home. That night, she took the pill, and slept really well.

The woman woke early in the morning feeling invigorated and refreshed. She ate a leisurely breakfast and arrived at work ten minutes ahead of time.

"As of this morning, my timekeeping problems are over," she happily announced to her boss.

"Well, that's good news," he said, "but where were you yesterday?"

Knock knock. Who's there?
Noah. Noah who?
Noah human who wants to play fetch?

More mysterious questions

What runs around the yard but never moves?
A fence.

Why did the man refuse to
buy a pocket calculator?
He already knew how many pockets he had.

What sits at the bottom
of the ocean and shudders?
A nervous wreck.

Slice of Life

A grandmother heard her grandchildren shouting in the kitchen, so she went in to find out what was wrong.

"What are you two fussing about now?" she asked. "My goodness, I wish you would learn to be more agreeable with each other."

"We are, grandma," Timmy answered. "Jenny thinks I'm not going to let her have any of the pie you baked, and I'm agreeing!"

Why did the baby cookie cry?
Because her mother was a wafer so long.

How do you fix a broken tomato?
With tomato paste.

Why did the apple go out with the fig?
It couldn't find a date.

What do we live for if it is not to make life
less difficult for each other?

George Eliot

*Everyone must have felt that a cheerful
friend is like a sunny day,
which sheds its brightness on all around.*

John Lubbock

The happiest conversation is that of which
nothing is distinctly remembered,
but a general effect of pleasing impression.

Samuel Johnson

That Sinking Feeling

Alice was on her first cruise, and once she lost sight of land, she became increasingly nervous. Spotting the captain, she rushed over to him and asked,

"Captain, do ships this size sink very often?"

"No, ma'am," the captain replied. "Never more than once."

Setting Sail

The ark was about to cast off. All the people and animals were finally aboard. As the creatures settled down in various parts of the boat, Noah noticed a look of concern on his wife's face.

"Are you worrying about the lions or the tigers?" Noah asked.

His wife shook her head.

"Are you afraid of the crocodiles or the boa constrictors?" he asked.

His wife said she wasn't.

"Well, is it the elephants or the rhinos that have you so anxious?" Noah continued.

"No," his wife answered.

"Well, tell me, what is it?" Noah asked.

His wife sighed. "I'd just feel a lot more relaxed if you'd put those termites in a jar."

Animal Arithmetic

After the rains stopped and dry land appeared, Noah opened the doors of the ark and told the animals to go forth and multiply.

All of them exited except for two snakes.

"Aren't you going to go forth and multiply?"

"We can't," the snakes replied. "We're adders."

Oh, all right. I'll wear the patch.
But I refuse to yo ho ho!

A person without a sense of humor
is like a wagon without springs—
jolted by every pebble in the road.

Henry Ward Beecher

Every step of the journey is the journey.

Proverb

Happiness is not a state to arrive at,
but rather, a manner of traveling.

Samuel Johnson

Life's a Bumpy Ride

Laughter is a lot like a car's shock absorbers—it helps get us over the potholes of life as smoothly as possible. Laughter is what cushions us against everything from bumpy moments to rough patches to wheel-spinning meltdowns.

We can't control every situation as we travel through life. We can't even be sure where we're going all the time. So we might as well laugh—and have people we care about along for the ride.

Fun on the Farm

A Texas farmer was visiting a farmer in the Midwest.

"So is this all your land?" the Texan asked.

"Yes, it's all mine," the Midwesterner replied.

"Really? This is all of it?" the Texan said with surprise.

"Yes, it is all mine!" the Midwestern farmer stated proudly.

"Well, to tell you the truth," said the Texan, "back home I'd get in my car at sunrise and I'd drive and drive and drive. By sunset, I'd only be halfway across my land!"

"Oh, that's too bad," replied the Midwesterner. "I used to have a car like that."

When does it rain money?
When there's a change in the weather.

Where do penguins keep their money?
In a snow bank.

What did the cat say when
he lost all his money?
I'm paw.

Banker's Special

Two bankers went into a diner and ordered two coffees. Then they took out sandwiches from their briefcases and started to eat.

The surprised waiter marched over and told them, "Sirs, you can't eat your own sandwiches in here!"

The bankers looked at each other, shrugged their shoulders and then exchanged sandwiches.

"What do you call a kitty
    cat who eats a duck?"
"I don't know."
"A duck-filled fatty puss!"
    "That is so not funny!"

If you would not be laughed at,
be the first to laugh at yourself.

Benjamin Franklin

Most folks are about as happy
as they make up their minds to be.

Abraham Lincoln

If you wish to glimpse inside a human soul
and get to know a man...
just watch him laugh.
If he laughs well, he's a good man.

Fyodor Dostoyevsky

Be happy. It's one way of being wise.

Colette

Learn how to feel joy.

Seneca

The world is a looking-glass
and gives back to every man
the reflection of his own face.
Frown at it and it will in turn
look sourly upon you;
laugh at it and with it,
and it is a jolly, kind companion.

William Makepeace Thackeray

Bumper Sticker Shock

- My reality check just bounced.

- If you can read this, my horse trailer is missing.

- A day without sunshine is – night.

- Give me ambiguity, or give me something else.

- Honk if you like peace and quiet.

- Watch out for the idiot behind me.

- Driver carries no cash. He is married.

- If you can read this, you are probably pulling me over.

I've Got Plans

Three mice were sitting around bragging about their strength, bravery, and prowess. The first mouse stood up and said, "Mouse traps? Pfft! They're nothing to me. In fact, I do push-ups with the bar while eating the cheese!"

The second mouse lazily reached inside his pocket and pulled out a capsule. "See this, guys?" He popped the pill into his mouth and swallowed it. "That was rat poison. I eat it for a snack."

The third mouse got up and headed for the door. "Hey, where do you think you're going?" the other two mice hollered.

"Time to get home," the third mouse said. "I haven't chased the cat yet today."

Why do mice need oiling?
They squeak.

Which mouse was a Roman emperor?
Julius Cheeser.

What does a twelve pound
mouse say to a cat?
"Here, kitty, kitty, kitty."

Under the Stars

Two brothers decided to camp out in the backyard on a hot summer night. The mosquitos wouldn't leave them alone, so they tried to hide from the insects by crawling into their sleeping bags.

After awhile, one of the boys peeked out and saw lightning bugs hovering all around.

"It's no use trying to hide from them, " the boy told his brother. "Now they brought flashlights."

How to Build a Campfire

Split a tree limb into smaller pieces.
Put a bandaid on your hand.
Keep chopping the pieces into smaller pieces.
Put a bandaid on your other hand.
Pile them all together.
Light a match.
Light a match.
Light a match.
Bend close and blow gently on the flames.
Put aloe on the burn on your nose.
Collect more wood.
When the fire is really going, add all the wood
that's left.
Wait while the unexpected storm passes.
Repeat above steps.

I'm feeling downy.
Anyone know a good joke?

Always Label Your Things

A cowboy lost his favorite Bible while he was out mending fences on the range. He looked everywhere but unfortunately, he couldn't find it.

Three weeks later, a duck waddled up to him carrying the Bible in its bill. The cowboy couldn't believe his eyes. He took the precious book out of the duck's mouth, raised his eyes heavenward and exclaimed, "It's a miracle!"

"Not really," said the duck. "Your name is written inside the cover."

Take Time to Laugh

We're all busy people in such a busy world. Yet the key to staying not only active, but productive, effective and happy, is relaxation. The time we give our body and soul, our head and heart to rest is crucial to maintaining mental and spiritual health.

If you feel you're too busy to take time out—even a little time every day—take it as a sign that you've got waaaay too much on your plate. Change what you can to give yourself what you need the most. For even a few minutes, savor the joy of having nothing to do but simply live, love and laugh!

**If you are too busy to laugh,
you are too busy.**

Proverb

*He that is of a merry heart hath
a continual feast.*

Proverbs 15:15

**A good laugh is the perfect way
to ventilate a stuffy day.**

Bested

Three boys were trying to best each other.

The first boasted, "My dad's a doctor.
I can get sick for nothing."

The second one countered. "My dad's a
lawyer, and I can get out of trouble for
nothing."

"You two don't have anything on me," the
third boy declared. "My dad is a policeman,
and I can be good for nothing."

Clearing Up Things

A dermatologist was surprised that the skin ointment she prescribed had failed to clear up a patient's rash.

"Have you been using it every day?" she asked.

"No, I couldn't," answered the patient.

"Why not?" the doctor inquired.

"Because it says 'apply locally', and I've been out of town all week."

Q: What do you call a pedicure for cats?
A: A PAWS for relaxation…

Many of us would probably
have become comedians,
if it weren't for having to
stand up so much.

*Stretch the truth far enough and you'll get a
snappy comeback.*

Laughter says everything
without saying a word.

Words to Live By

- Interchangeable parts usually aren't.

- Those who keep calm in a crisis have no idea what's going on.

- Just because the label says "one size fits all" doesn't mean it will fit you.

- For every little action, there's bound to be an overreaction.

- They say it's a small, small world, but I still wouldn't want to dust it.

- There are many yoga pants that have never been to yoga.

"Knock knock."

   "Who's there?"

"Gopher."

   "Gopher who?"

"Gopher a toy, okay? I'm really bored!"

All's Well

Two pigeons agreed that they would meet for a date on the ledge outside the ninth floor of an office building. The gal pigeon was at the appointed place right on time, but her guy was nowhere in sight. As the minutes passed, she became increasingly distraught, imagining all the horrible things that could have happened to her friend.

Half an hour later, her guy appeared on the ledge. Breathing a sigh of relief, she asked him where he had been all this time.

"Oh, it was such a nice day," the guy pigeon answered, "so I decided to walk."

What do you call a parrot that flies away?
Polygon.

Why did the little bird
get in trouble at school?
He was caught tweeting on a test.

Why did Mozart sell his chickens?
Because they kept saying
"Bach bach bach Bach"!

Shopping Spree

A woman ran into an old co-worker hurrying down the sidewalk one day.

"Hi," he said. "Been out shopping?"

"Yes, I have," the woman replied.

"Whenever I'm down in the dumps, I get new clothes," he smiled. Then he went on his way.

Hmmm. I always wondered where he got his clothes, she said to herself.

What did the shoes say to the hat?
You go on a head. I'll follow you on foot.

Fashion designers are just so clothes-minded.

Some women have two complaints:
*Nothing to wear and not enough
closet space.*

How much did the pirate
pay for his earrings?
A buccaneer!

Laugh and the world laughs with you.
Cry and you'll have to do
your make-up all over again.

Why did the girl bring blush
and eye shadow to school?
She had a make-up exam!

Why did the woman put
lipstick on her forehead?
She was trying to make up her mind.

*Don't know why,
but I'm in the mood
for some hog and dogs ice cream*

Bravery Above and Beyond

Three guys were sitting around boasting about their experiences. One fellow told about how he had crawled under a house to retrieve a neighbor's boa constrictor.

The next guy reported that he had once tackled a vicious dog that had a little old lady cornered.

"Well, I can top both of those stories," the third man said. "I came face to face with a lion once, and he was headed right at me!"

"Wow, what did you do?" his buddies gasped.

"Well, I tried standing still and looking him straight in the eye, but he kept coming at me. Then I tried moving backward verrrrrry slowly, but he started moving faster in my direction.

"So how did you finally get away?" said his friends, impressed with his courage.

"I turned around, bought a hot dog and went to another part of the zoo."

Dieters Speak Out

"I'm serious about losing weight.
I always have a diet soda with
my doughnut."

"Dieting made me tired, so I bought some of
those drinks that give you energy.
You know what happened? I ate faster."

"Do you call someone who
abandons her diet a desserter?"

"I'm in shape. Round is a shape."

Confidence

One day a woodpecker was pecking a hole in a large oak tree. Suddenly the sky darkened, the wind rose up and a streak of lightning sent the oak tree toppling to the ground.

"Wow!" exclaimed the astonished woodpecker. "I guess I didn't know my own strength!"

Why don't chickens like people?
They beat eggs.

What do you call a rooster who wakes you
up at the same time every morning?
An alarm cluck.

Why does a chicken coop have two doors?
If it had four doors,
it would be a chicken sedan.

Why yes, I am a practical yolker!
(I crack me up sometimes.)

Name Dropping

Two women were waiting quite awhile for the elevator. To break the silence, the younger one, who was rather nervous, said, "That new boss is a dingbat!"

The other glanced at her and said, "Hello. I don't believe we've met before. Do you know who I am?"

When the first shook her head, the other winked and whispered, "I'm the dingbat's wife."

The young woman took a deep breath.

"Well, do you know who I am?" she inquired.

The boss's wife shook her head.

"Good!" shouted the young woman as she ran for the stairs.

Work Wisdom

Every Friday afternoon at 4:45, the boss called a staff meeting. Finally, one of his employees got up the courage to ask him why he always had the meeting fifteen minutes before the start of the weekend.

"Easy," the boss replied. "It's the only time I can be sure that no one's going to spend time arguing with what I say."

Law and Order

On his first day on the job, the rookie police officer noticed a group of people loitering on a street corner. Wanting to impress his supervisor, he pulled out his bullhorn and began to yell, "Okay, everyone. Break it up. Move along. Go back to your homes now, please."

One by one, the group dispersed, everyone looking puzzled and worried.

"So how did I do?" the officer asked his supervisor.

"Not bad, I guess, considering this is a bus stop."

Put More Funny in Your Life

- Hang out more often with funny friends and relatives.

- Visit the humor section of your local bookstore.

- Invite folks over for a game night. (No serious competition, though!)

- Memorize a funny story to keep on hand just in case.

- Install a funny app on your phone— or ask your kid to!

- Turn your living room into a comedy club and invite family members to make up routines. (The cornier the better.)

- Get out some old photos of you and show your kids.

- Be on the lookout for unexpected chances to not take yourself so seriously.

- Commit a random act of laughter today.

A good laugh is a mighty good thing,
and rather too scarce a good thing.

Herman Melville

Remember this: very little is needed
to make a happy life.

Marcus Aurelius

I have learned, in whatsoever state I am,
therewith to be content.

Philippians 4:11

The Case of the Slipping Comma

While rushing around, a pastor glanced at a note sent to him by Mrs. Schultz, one of his parishioners. The note read: "Bill Schultz, having gone to sea, his wife desires prayers for his safety."

Later, during prayer requests, the pastor remembered the note and announced to the congregation: "Bill Schultz, having gone to see his wife, desires prayers for his safety."

Don't mean to be nosey,
but I've been wondering,
what makes YOU laugh??